BLOOD
LYRICS

Books by Katie Ford

Deposition
Storm (chapbook)
Colosseum
Blood Lyrics

BLOOD LYRICS

Poems

KATIE FORD

Graywolf Press

This publication is made possible, in part, by the voters of Minnesota through a Minnesota State Arts Board Operating Support grant, thanks to a legislative appropriation from the arts and cultural heritage fund, and through grants from the National Endowment for the Arts and the Wells Fargo Foundation Minnesota. Significant support has also been provided by Target, the McKnight Foundation, Amazon.com, and other generous contributions from foundations, corporations, and individuals. To these organizations and individuals we offer our heartfelt thanks.

Published by Graywolf Press
250 Third Avenue North, Suite 600
Minneapolis, Minnesota 55401

www.graywolfpress.org

Published in the United States of America

ISBN 978-1-55597-692-7

2 4 6 8 9 7 5 3 1
First Graywolf Printing, 2014

Library of Congress Control Number: 2014935705

Cover design: Jeenee Lee Design

Cover photo: *After Hasegowa Tōhaku* (left panels of five panel image),
        archival pigment print, 18 x 60 inches (total),
        by Scott Wright © 2010, scottwrightartwork.com.

for my daughter

Contents

Coda

BLOOD
LYRICS

I run to the gates and rattle them —
just tell me what will happen —

a few sad beasts come forward,
but as for the oracle, the oracle
will not come forward.

I.

BLOODLINE

A Spell

Take my lights, take my most and only opal,
take the thin call of bells I hear,
just. Take that thin lead,
wring out my water and drink
the wrung remains, take all that is nimble
and sun-up of day,
break my window to steal my eyes,
take their cotton, reap their fields;
as for my industry, it is yours.
I know in wishing not to bluff
so lay me on a threshing floor
and bleed me in the old, slow ways,
but do not take my child.

Of a Child Early Born

For the child is born an unbreathing scripture
and her broken authors wait
on one gurney together.
And what is prayer from a gurney
but lantern-glow for God or demon
to fly toward the lonely in this deathly hour,
and since I cannot bear to wish on one
but receive the other,
I lie still, play dead, am delivered decree:
our daughter weighs seven hundred dimes,
paperclips, teaspoons of sugar,
this child of grams
for which the good nurse
laid out her studies
as a coin purse
into which our tiny wealth clinked,
our daughter spilling almost
to the floor.
You cannot serve God and wealth
but I'll serve my wealth and live,
yes, and be struck dead
if lightning staggers down the hall of mothers—
and it does,
        so walk low, mothers,
fresh from your labors.

Trivial

Trivial the land, trivial the blue.
And the sea, too:
trivial the fight with the trivial.

The garden plot wasted at the gate
worked by scratch and spade, trivial—
seed of spiked grass and leek,
the finch roiled inside
so trivial to me.

Era, caves, cliff-side, creed,
planked corners of the broken mind,
trivial now where I am beside
my only fact:

the one I love is sick.
There is no break
but the one break.

Children's Hospital

Our sorrow had neither place nor carrier-away,
and dared not hover over the child
whose breath opened as transom
of a frail house.
Nor could we put sorrow in the dictionary,
for *ghastliness* already shot out its own defining
in rags of fired light.
Pigeons would not sleek it
over their dirty feathers, nor fly
sorrow against the coop's sharp fence.
Each day bridgeless, each night birdless,
all the nocturnals huddled against
the hidden weight of snow.
        But wake at the moon,
we could, mumbling, *are we*
in a horror show? —inside of sleep
our shock-white minds caught on reels
where a child's body breaks the heart
and the mother can't know
if she counts as a mother. I don't know
if the child heard
what wept at the bedside,
orderlies snapping smelling salts
from chalky bullets against
all the mothers falling,
all the fathers under
what each branch let down.
        The earth, so shaken,
shook.

[O where has our meadow gone?
that which swept us here?
the orange cosmos and aster?
the hollycock and pollen-fire?

So I sing of hell
and the brutal body.]

Sleep and Her Ache

Both flew brightly
to my bed

I nightmared
far from her

my body
her empty tomb

all the while
the earth laid down
its brutal head
it would not lament

it might be prudent
if it could not detect me

with the sound of sighs
I slept lightly then

Condition

Lead versus feathers, feathers
versus months of thunderous metal,
wherefore she hums,
no measure of her ready
but this measure, a humming, a tone
as winter drags its torpored era here,
steady as iron is unbending and bronzed,
hindered badly she unhindered hums,
so unworried her sounds
through dangers hundreds and believable
with feathers neither swift enough
nor bird enough nor feather through
and through. While winter
rakes and stones,
softly unbelievable she hums.

Little Torch

There should have been delight, delight
and windchimes, delight.
But she was clawing the beach
after so much battering,
a torch lit past the slim pine pitch
and draw of resin she was dipped in
at the beginning of the earth.

They said life might flee—
then tended the creature as if a torch,
bundling reeds tightly as day torched
toward them,
soaking rags in lime and sulfur
around barely lit bone.

Such are the wonders I saw.

Song of the Thimble

Here is the whiskey taken down from my cupboard.
It tastes of caramel and heat and miners and sea.
Maybe a mother with love long on the brink
will knock at my door to talk of tubes, taps, fusions,
to say yes-mine-lived-yours-might-too.
But there's no such knock tonight.

I pour just a thimble
(clean milk is due the nurse by dawn)
and drink what will not grow thin.
Again in my mind
I pour it, I pour it, I drink.

Upon Waking

When I woke up sighing, perceiving myself in the freeze,
perceiving my body in the terrifying orchard, sighing
and contending, contending and appearing, disappear-
ing into sighing, sighing of ornament and cargo, pull-
ing down what was broken from twilight and broken
from dawn, perceiving what in sleep only strengthened
its contention, though I mistook night as healer, sleep as
erasure, vespers as lumbering dissolution toward mat-
ins, matins a leaf made violet since it hangs askance
grapes in sun, since I mistook the leaf for myself, corre-
lating and equating, the determined danger given water
and meat, when the mistake pulled down and I woke
not arisen but sighing, sighing so the ornaments knew I
was nothing to hang upon, no shuttle to loom by, when
I could not make a word and the given words of each
book failed me into sighing, it was then, to live, I had
to say *yes*.

The Soul

It disappeared.
It reappeared
as chimney smoke
burning through carcasses
of swallows stilled,
and that it portrayed no will
was why I followed that smoke
with this pair of eyes.

It was that it didn't need
or require
my belief
that I leant upon it
as a tired worker
upon
a gate.

Snow at Night

I prefer it even to love,
alone and without ghost
it falls a hard weather,
a withdrawing room
that revives me to stolen daylight
in which I feel no wish
to brush a gleaming finish
over the sheen-broken glass
I've arranged and rearranged,
an apprentice of mosaics
who will not be taught but asks
to be left alone with the brittle year
so carnivorous of all I'd made.
But the snow I love covers
my beasts and seas,
my ferns and spines
worn through and through.
I will change your life, it says,
to which I say *please*.

The Fire

When a human is asked about a particular fire,
she comes close:
then it is too hot,
so she turns her face—

and that's when the forest of her bearable life appears,
always on the other side of the fire. The fire
she's been asked to tell the story of,
she has to turn from it, so the story you hear
is that of pines and twitching leaves
and how her body is like neither—

all the while there is a fire
at her back
which she feels in fine detail,
as if the flame were a dremel
and her back its etching glass.

You will not know all about the fire
simply because you asked.
When she speaks of the forest
this is what she is teaching you,

you who thought you were her master.

[Tell me it's April,
tell me you live into a little girl,
when I tip you back to lay you down
your breath remains and keeps remaining,
tell me the morning trucks delivered bread
to the market while we were sleeping,
that the newspaper is flung against our door,
tell me it woke us, it is Sunday, all we have to do is
reach outside, in it comes! and open it—]

That It Is Even Possible to Stay Alive

The massive inner life of ice
descends over the violet newborn
of this city. The open-mouthed statues
of the winter fountain, the tourist horses
stomping their hollow bones,
the apple-skins and feathers.
O see it try to break our world.

But if a hundred years ago influenza
almost took this city,
if tags were tied to toes when patients
were carried into the wards—
if they said *but I'm still living*
as the horrified doctors covered themselves away—

then, my love, we should wake
to each other and ransack
this flushed skin of everything
but praise.

Mathematician

In that tight-sheltered ghost
of quiet I keep,
I count her more dearly
than any genesis night
when the first dark fell
and the father reckoned up
the world. How I count
is day in and out
and without end.
I need no sabbath
from the count
seated in my closed, open,
half-shut eyes.
Strange we must be
to the maker who made us
less weary in love than he.

Song after Sadness

Despair is still servant
to the violet and wild ongoings
of bone. You, remember, are
that which must be made
servant only to salt, only
to the watery acre that is the body
of the beloved, only to the child
now leaning forward into
the exhibit of birches
the forest has made of bronze light
and snow. Even as the day kneels
forward, the oceans and strung garnets, too,
kneel, they all kneel,
the city, the goat, the lime tree
and mother, the fearful doctor,
kneel. Don't say it's the beautiful
I praise. I praise the human,
gutted and rising.

Blood Lyric

I come to you without wound
and in the strength of my life.
Heaven cannot touch me; neither can the earth.
In this clear field, the stripped birch does not represent me,
thus I give back the respect I once stole.
I give back its own life trying to break through
the low canopy draped like an abandoned wedding tent.

I am without wound, but this is a small slat
I speak through and briefly.
By the end of these words, strength
might be gone, new pain come, old pains returned
as elderly selves grown quiet
with the knowledge of what did
and did not happen.

Long live such confidence as I have these five minutes now.
Long live the primate's human eyes inside of the cage.
Long live the surgeon steady enough
to examine the bloody heart beating in his hands
before the minutes are up
and it must be put back
inside.

II.

our LONG war

To Read of Slaughter

Some things qualify as silence, but wake us
like the disappearance of birdcall that kept us asleep
because we took it as dream-stitch
or the early steps of the beloved lighting the stove
until we wake only when the stove
remains unlit against the day
now bewildering each hibernation,
each lightly drugged feather, each stun and lie.

The Throats of Guantánamo

Morning opens with the comforts of my unbeaten body
a tinkerer's stack of quiltings and cannings the cloth finch

half-attached to a mobile of warblers and wrens
in the meantime my country sends post to mothers and fathers

back again fly a trinity of boys
with their throats cut out

simultaneity drinks twig tea and stitches
a hidden seam

I take a string to a bittern's back and tie it
to the looping newborn delight

then read of each strangulation no bone or larynx
for proof maybe each part was tossed to bay

a medieval saint was asked what would you do if you knew
it was the end of the world

I'd dig in my garden he said
oh saint it's a good answer

but here the end is torn out
one by one.

[We're here because we're here because
we're here, because we're here
We're here because we're here because
we're here, because we're here
         I hear the young scouts a-singing.]

Song of the Damned

I was trying to remember the songs of the valley
shouting to the hilltops, streams and meadows rushing—
but something banned me from such songs. Something
wanted me to resign from praise,
perhaps for my whole life,
perhaps past my life
into the banishment
of the far, blind eternity.

What can I do? I have seen vineyards and orange groves
rise after seasons of sudden freeze.
The markets in my town burst with avocado, grain, ale,
sweet alyssum sold in handfuls. Yet gratitude
is not allowed me, not without offense.
Not in my country.

Our Long War

If we are at war let the orchards show it,
let the pear and fig fall prior to their time,
let the radios die
and the hounds freeze over their meat,
let the balconies crack their planked backs as we recline,
let the streets of stock and trade split open,
let the horses pulling at the fields
wither beneath us.

Let each year decay and each decade:

to receive report is not enough,
equations of the mathematician must
each come wrong, strangely, inexplicably, the remedies
must run dry,
the violet must let no more tincture
and the waters no more cool.
When, at mudtimes, we trek to the waterfall,
there it should no longer be—
nothing should fall where the guidebook says,
not orchids, not taro,
not the market, not the fishmonger thrashing carp against rock
where once we bought it bloody on the board.

If we are at war with a holy book in our hands
let it shrivel to slag; its teachings
cannot survive the drone
and will not gleam while villagers drink the ditch.

If we wage it, let the war breach up
into the light, let it unseam our garments
where they hold fast, let each button and string fail
until we run to hide ourselves

in alleys where at least rats and refuse
and the sleeping poor show some partial ghost
of what's abroad.

If we war there ought to be a sign.
Our lives should feel like cut-outs of lives,
paper dolls drifting to the ground,
ready for chalk outlines.

But still our horses ripple their flanks
and the orange grove shakes green in the warm wind it loves.
We laze on the balcony with clear water in the glass.
At the newsstand stacks of cigarettes
with their sure wrappings and that little red pull, candies and juices
made of wild thriving corn.
In winter we ornament fountains with Christmas lights,
in spring more falsely, and more falsely,
the scent of heather and sedge grows rich through the transom.

Before the war
the soul
spoke so clearly
we took it for an imbecile.

But now the war can't know what it wants:
we make meals, pay a tax, and dream nothing
hard enough to wake us.

Not once have I dreamt of the war.
I forgot it quietly, unwantingly, and because
there were peaches everywhere, peaches
that shouldn't have happened,
nor the idea of blessing at sundown,
the orchard lit into an avenue
of torchlight.

Still Life

Down by the pond, addicts sleep
on rocky grass half in water, half out,
and there the moon lights them
out of tawny silhouettes into the rarest
of amphibious flowers I once heard called *striders,*
between, but needing, two worlds.
Of what can you accuse them now,
                              beauty?

Immigrant Hospital

Bobigny

Chalky as white spruce
in hill fog pressed away from Sacre Coeur,
not one in seventy tongues
that make love acute and possessed are speaking now
their dozens of faiths and doubts. Just chrome whisperings,
endearments. Still, the priest of these wards must know
which voice, which prayer,
which he finds eases. Which unfolds
a rope ladder from this housefire, which will not
sleep but comes into the metal bed
after the nurses go and chants your own secret
incompletion into death. All I want, I said,
is to know this.
                    Visit the sick, he answered.

Makeshift Hospital

Baghdad

Night—
the common hours
for loosened souls
to be hastened into the kingdom
of unspecified light.

Theory of War

Admit coming upon the fallen horse at evening,
now asleep but withered, now reducing as you near, now
a dell pony at your feet beneath the alder dead,
admit it is too much to both see and bear. You must
either not see or not bear, or see and bear
some quickened portion, the portion allotted to say
this is simply the field
of what occurs on earth.

The Lord Is a Man of War

The Lord is a man of war
I read by window and wick

and for once I believed
the book of Exodus true
the origin of our points sharpened
with fire our axes bows our pikes

and finally I could see
the cooling lava pits of their eyes
their giant gingko ears
their bellows of desert pain
how elephants became elephantry

how the woman who fevered with pox
became after death a weapon
a contagion to catapult over fortified walls

and finally I knew
why in this theater
the missiles are named
Savage Sinner Scapegoat
Peacekeeper and Goblet

Herren er en stridsmann
my descent is of the Vikings so
man is a Lord of war.

[Here is the board, here the water.
Baptism is as bad as they say:
you must renounce the devil
you never met.]

Far Desert Region

Comes August, comes December,
then April thinned of its birds.
Again August, ten times.
Fathers forage the bombed chemical plant
for barrels to carry water
from the lime-bright pools to houses
leaning inside hot wind.

To think a war might give a gift:
a pool, a clean bucket.

Remedies for Sorrow

                    The soldierly ready
of human sadness: it must, by nature, hover.
I water the date palm at dawn in the desert acre. I can see
it's not alive; the landscape doesn't need me. This is May,
May should riffle pollen toward another,
women should weave fans of stiff reeds
to sweep air palm to palm, but my friend says he just tries
to keep his body busy. Sunday a horror movie,
Tuesday the opera, Thursday tea with the reclusive poet
who comes out just for him. He is an audience to the arts
of extremity in the apartment that gilds itself
a mean irony of light.
Time passes, is the early summer squash.
He asks the farmer how he cooks it—
I scoop the seeds and cut butter and nutmeg
into its little boat—
but at the end of each living task
there is a fringe of loss.
The heart works hard at the apprenticeship
of a diligent hand learning to pull
wet porcelain into a thinness of wall
just prior to what's brittle. We talked of remedies
last week on the phone—can you swim the bay,
I ask, take in the cats, put up the Japanese shades,
trace your life in pins? The loss of love will
try it all.
                    Dear merchant of a twice-stolen boat,
when surgeons cut deeply
into the dark matter, you said, I believe
we can be made whole again.
What did you mean, *again?*

November Philosophers

Nothing is nothing, although
he would call me that, *she was nothing.*
Those were his words, but his hand was lifting
cigarettes in chains and bridges
of ash-light. He said he didn't want his body to last.
It wasn't a year I could argue
against that kind of talk, so I cut the fowl
killed on the farm a mile out—brown and silvery, wild—
and put it over butter lettuce, lettuce then lime.
I heated brandy in the saucepan, poured a strip of molasses
slowly through the cold, slow as I'd seen
a shaman pour pine tincture over the floor
of my beaten house.
She seemed to see my whole life
by ordinance of some god
who wanted me alive again.
Burnt sage, blue smoke. Then sea salt shaken
into the corners of violent sadness.
She wrote my address
across her chest
to let everything listening know
where my life was made.
We waited, either forgetting what we were
or becoming more brightly human in that pine,
in her trance, in the lavender I set on the chipped sills,
not a trance at all but my deliberate hand cutting
from the yard part of what she required.
Now wait longer, she said, and I did as I would
when the molasses warmed over the pot enough
to come into the brandy,
to come into the night
begun by small confessions—

that this was just a rental, and mine just a floor,
that the woman he loved was with another man,
his mother mad, his apartment haunted in the crawl space.
Then I told of the assault at daybreak between
the houses. Heat, asphalt, all of it and my face toward
the brick school where the apostolate studied first-century script
and song. There must have been chanting,
as it was on the hour.
What we said was liturgy meant only for us
and for that night. Not for anyone else
to repeat, live by, believe. Never that.
Our only theories were inside of our hands,
flesh and land, body and prairie.
I reached to smoke down his next-to-last,
which he lit and made ready.
The poultry like a war ration
we ate all the way through.
What we wished, we said.
What we said, we found that night
by these, and no other,
means.

[Does the war want
us to unstitch its side and climb in, to become
its good surgeon?
                    Stupid poet, a war can't know
                    what it wants.]

BLOOD LYRICS

43

Beasts of the Field

Name those things, too,
you cannot bear the thinking of.
In blackberries and moths Adam drew up a study:
carpet bombs, drones, solitary.
So it behooved God not to create these.

[Savage, Sinner, Scapegoat, Peacekeeper,
Exdrone, Blue Streak, Fireflash.
Long March, Peacekeeper, Gladiator, Grail,
Theatre, Scrooge, Gimlet, Wasserfall,
Blue Eye, Peacekeeper, Patriot, Ash.]

Pistol

He put pistol shadow
where my husband's hand had been,
pistol now in hand as shadow,
but unlike any good shadow
of linden or grass, portioned
according to fresh light as it passed,
no time could erase this portion,
no hand could loose such shadow.
Husband, I said, *look at my hand.*
He stared at what a stranger
had put by crime on skin, my land.
I put ideas, camphor, soils in hand
but the pistol only grew
and having little left to lose, I said
give me back my mind to know
if this is now my steely hand
in which he left such shadow.

Little Belief

By this river wall
this solvent light
it's stark enough to say
I hate, I think,

I think in the quartz
the water sharpens back
how badly
I would like to have
a cutting tool,
a proven gun.

A heavy work
it must have been
to strip this river of film
so I can say,

there are humans
the worst of dogs
put to shame.

Mercy, have mercy on me.

Shooting Gallery

A shooting gallery!
I step right up:
ten paper men
smile at me
and circle round and round.

O my pellet!
It tears a hole
clean through!

My olde-tymey men,
such steadfast smiles
make happy practice!

          I could get used to us.

Sighting

I did not see a god,
and the god I did not see was not
the god I was told
to see or call, alternately,
in the trade and settle of God's country
where the farmer's root crops
were gone, almost—

Shoot me, said the earth,
like a woman who would not
do it to herself. The ones who heard
convinced her why not, why not
even as they took their sticks
to her in the street.

Shoot me, said the earth. *Shoot.*

Little Goat

God is not light upon light, no more
than goat is need upon need,
although there, where it grazes, it is sun upon coat
within which ticks and stray-blown feed burrow
into the pocked skin of such foul scent
covering the underflesh heart that could eat
this farmer's grain or the barren mountain's bark
high in the solitude of sheer animal peace
laid over sheer animal terror.

We ask the animal afflicted by its time,
its impoverished American meadow
that drove it to find birch from which to strip its easy feed
to abide with us.
It does not need us. We think it needs us.
We must forgive God God's story.

The Day-Shift Sleeps,

the night-war wakes:
Torturers button their canvas shirts.
They straighten their cots.
They bite their toast.
They tidy their folders.
They smoke their smokes.
They tidy their blank, blank folders.
All the little chores
before going on a trip,
theirs is the zeal of children.

Foreign Song

To bomb them,
we mustn't have heard their music
or known their waterless night watch,
we mustn't have seen how already
the desert was under constant death bells
ringing over sleeping cribs and dry wells.
We couldn't have wanted
this eavesdropping
of names we've never pronounced
praying themselves toward death.

I try to believe in us —
we must not
have heard
their music.

[Tuesday wind brings a letter
from a friend: *Don't be naïve.*]

Choir

I once believed in heavenly clarity—
do you know how good it feels to sing
of certainty, the wild apricot
of the heart orange, large, full of reach
at day's unlatch?
Inside the mouth, certainty
is a fruit breaking apart.
That is how good it feels:
we would have despised anyone
to keep our song.

[How can God bear it,
the sound of our florid voices, thankful
for the provisions at our table—]

The Four Burns of the Soul

Whether something outside of us can reach in and affect change, aside or beside, beside or thinly away, thinly and unbearably so, God: this is the whether or whether not we cannot know. Whether to believe there is an unbearable distance or to imagine no distance, thereby feeling a proximity lifting oneself into that which is both imagined and is, or is imagined and is not, or not imagined and is, or not imagined and is not. Those are the choices, four. So that is the pain, that choosing is the only region for us. Here where the fires so constantly alternate their burns.

Choose an Instrument

Bells, bells,
              choose an instrument, fall
over antelope in the blue-green cemetery, cemetery,
choose, use yourself, ironworks, scrolls, doubt, body,

make an instrument of your broken lung,
learn landmines, train in the sensitive, immaculate technique
until less skin tears away, won't you choose,
your loss has made you immune and overwhelming,

into the rice field you wade, able, use yourself
to the night seeding of grain, pull tinctures,
fatten string nets against disease,
someone — photograph the massacre,

you are the canopy, the reed boat, the softly, long-sanded chair.
No one is chosen,
              choose.

coda

From the Nursery

After a while, I stopped asking whether my child would survive,
although everything I asked in its stead
could be heard as this question.

Her body, not ready for the bare earth,
and like a nude soul, suffered each thing
with an intuition impossibly more acute
than what her body could carry out
in practice.

I must have seemed, at times, almost unconcerned
by what the clinicians said—
each small, survivable diagnosis touched me only as the sleeve
of a passing stranger.

When I looked up from her hospital crib
to see the wider world, could I help it
if I saw a war?

I can sense you are poised to accuse me now
of that sentimental watershed we call new motherhood:

Because my child was threatened, I too quickly conclude
from my single-mindedness that no one should be threatened,
that we shouldn't kill
those asleep in their bedclothes
somewhere we haven't heard of, somewhere
foreign, a desert—an infant, a mother, many cousins.

I concede, it was an emotional time.
I felt I had been dropped from a considerable height
where the future remained, as it always had been,
stridently unknown; it was simply the pitch that had changed.

Now I look out from the nursery window—
first a birch tree, then rowhomes, the city, the country, the world—
still the war widens, wide as a prehistoric mouth,
wide as desperate slander.

If you wish, call me what the postpartum have long been called:
tired mother, overprotective bear,
open sore,
a body made sensitive
to the scent of fire or fume,
just as your mother would have been
when you were born, you who are alive
to read this now.

Notes

Chapter I., "Bloodline," is dedicated to Tristan and to Ronan, in memoriam.

"Children's Hospital": Matthew 6:24: "You cannot serve God and money."

"The Fire": a dremel is a tool used for etching and engraving glass.

"The Throats of Guantánamo" is based, in part, on Scott Horton's article, "The Guantánamo 'Suicides': A Camp Delta Sergeant Blows the Whistle" (*Harper's*, March 2010).

"We're Here Because We're Here" is a traditional American scout song sung to the tune of "Auld Lang Syne." It is written here in its entirety. The instruction for the song is to "Repeat until you get tired."

"The Lord Is a Man of War": Exodus 15:3: "The LORD is a man of war; the LORD is his name." *Herren er en stridsmann* translates, in Norwegian, as "The Lord is a man of war."

"Remedies for Sorrow" is for D. A. Powell.

"[Savage, Sinner, Scapegoat, Peacekeeper]": all words of this poem are the names of missiles and drones.

"From the Nursery": November 19, 2005, Haditha, Iraq: twenty-four unarmed Iraqi civilians were killed by United States Marines following the detonation of a roadside bomb that killed Lance Corporal Miguel Terrazas.

Acknowledgments

The author thanks the *Academy of American Poets, Bayou, Blackbird, Great River Review, Little Seal,* the *New Yorker, Pleiades, Plume, Poetry, Seneca Review, Smartish Pace, Tongue,* and the *Virginia Quarterly Review* for first publishing the individual poems of *Blood Lyrics,* often in very different forms.

"Our Long War" and "Still Life" were set to music by composer David Ludwig of the Curtis Institute of Music. "Still Life" (for soprano and piano) premiered in Chicago in 2013. "Our Long War" (for soprano, violin, and piano) premiered at the Lake Champlain Music Festival in 2011, and has since been performed in Philadelphia, Lubbock, Oklahoma City, Seoul, and Carnegie Hall, New York.

Gratitude to the Lannan Foundation, Franklin & Marshall College, and Alan L. Yudell for generous funding and support during the composition of this volume. Thank you: Louise Glück, Jay Hopler, Katy Howard, Ilya Kaminsky, Susan Lynch, Jesse Nathan, Katie Peterson, D. A. Powell, Sarah Sentilles, Jeff Shotts, Mary Szybist, and Nate Walker. But surpassingly, Josh. And perpetually, Maggie.

KATIE FORD is the author of *Deposition* and *Colosseum*, which was named a "Best Book of 2008" by *Publishers Weekly* and by the *Virginia Quarterly Review*. Her work has appeared in the *New Yorker*, the *Paris Review, Poetry*, and *Poetry International*. Her honors include a Lannan Literary Fellowship and the Larry Levis Reading Award. She teaches in the Department of Creative Writing at the University of California, Riverside, and lives with the writer Josh Emmons and their daughter.

Book design by Rachel Holscher. Composition by BookMobile Design & Digital Publisher Services, Minneapolis, Minnesota. Manufactured by Versa Press on acid-free, 30 percent postconsumer wastepaper.